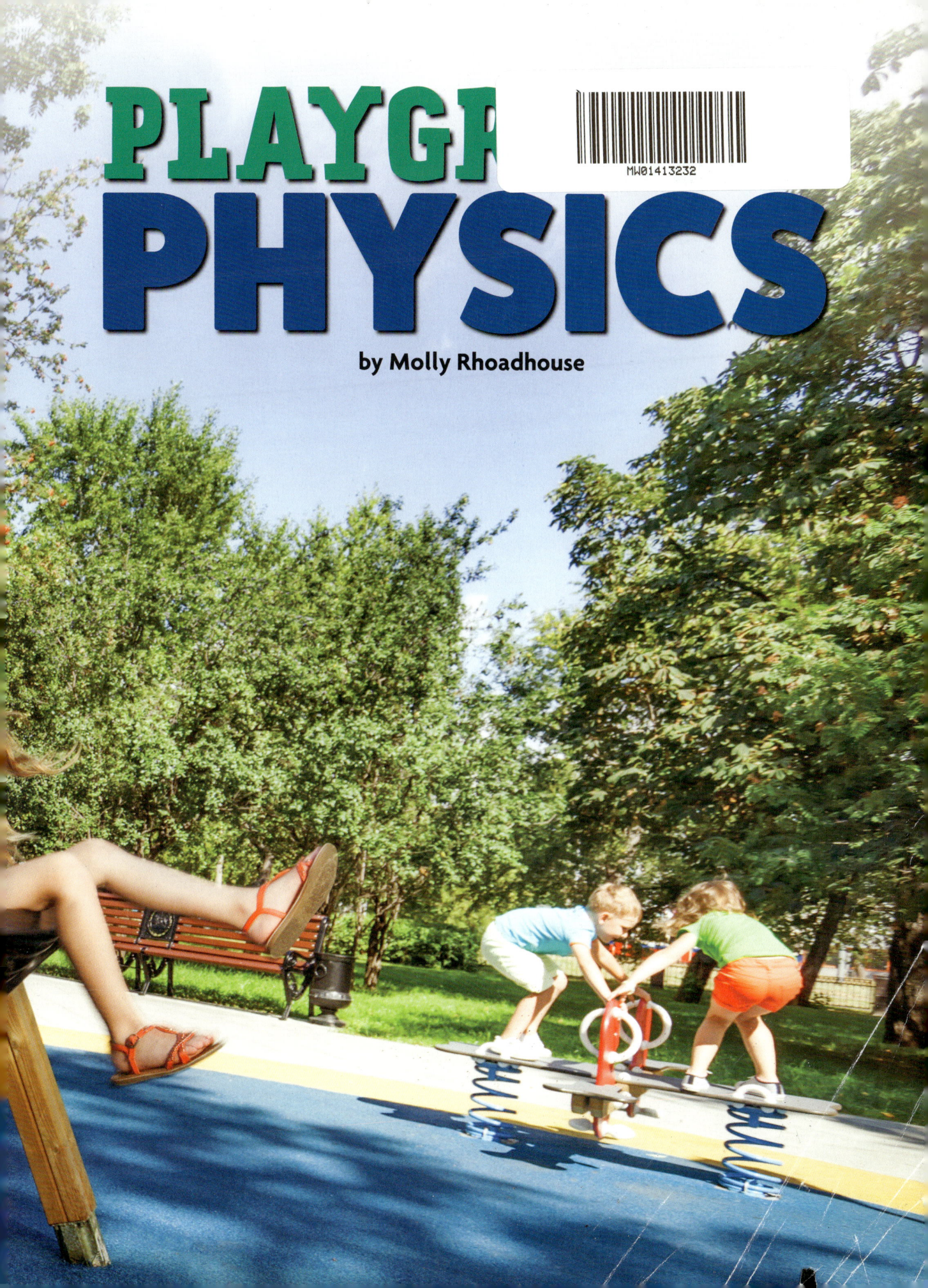

PLAYGROUND PHYSICS

by Molly Rhoadhouse

TABLE OF CONTENTS

Kick the Ball! 4
Playground Patterns 12
Meet a Playground Designer 18
Glossary/Index 24

KICK THE BALL!
Forces at Play

A kickball rolls and bounces slowly toward the kicker. She swings her leg and kicks the ball. In an instant, the ball is sailing overhead!

Forces in Kickball

Anytime a kickball changes its motion or speed, it is because of forces. Even when the ball is still, forces are acting on it.

The pitcher holds the ball still. But he is exerting a force on the ball. His hands are pushing the ball upward, so it doesn't fall to the ground.

Forces

Forces make a ball change direction and speed during a game. Forces are pushes or pulls that act on an object, such as a ball. Forces can cause changes in an object's motion.

A force is applied to a ball when it is thrown, kicked, or caught. Forces act on a ball when it flies in the air and rolls on the ground, too.

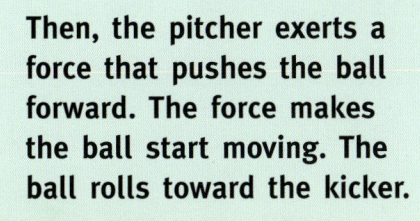

| Then, the pitcher exerts a force that pushes the ball forward. The force makes the ball start moving. The ball rolls toward the kicker. | Kicking the ball is an example of a type of force called a push. | The push makes the ball change the direction in which it is moving. This force changes the speed of the ball. |

5

Strength and Direction

Some kicks send a ball flying over the heads of other players. Some kicks move the ball only a short distance. Some kicks send the ball in one direction. Other kicks send the ball in another direction. What causes these differences? The differences are caused by the strength and the direction of the force.

Strength

The strength of a force tells how much the force pushes or pulls an object. The stronger a force, the more it can change an object's motion. A ball kicked with less force will not move as far as one kicked with a greater force.

Direction

The direction of a force tells which way the object is pushed or pulled. When a pitcher's arm moves back to pitch a ball, the force pulls the ball backward. When the pitcher tosses the ball, the force pushes the ball forward.

All forces have strength and direction

In diagrams that explain forces, an arrow shows the strength of a force. The longer the arrow, the bigger the force. The arrow also shows the direction of the force.

What would happen if two kids playing soccer kicked the ball at the same time in the same direction? The ball would move faster and farther than if only one player had kicked it.

When two forces act in the same direction, they combine and make the force bigger. The forces can be added together to find the total force acting on the object. The total force acting on an object is called the net force.

Two Forces Are Greater Than One!

Tony is pushing a heavy box of softball bats and gloves across the infield. Pushing as hard as he can, he is able to move the box only a short distance. But when a friend helps him push, the box moves more easily. This is because the force Tony's friend applies to the box is added to the force Tony applies. If each person pushes with the same force, then two people can push the box with twice as much force as one person alone.

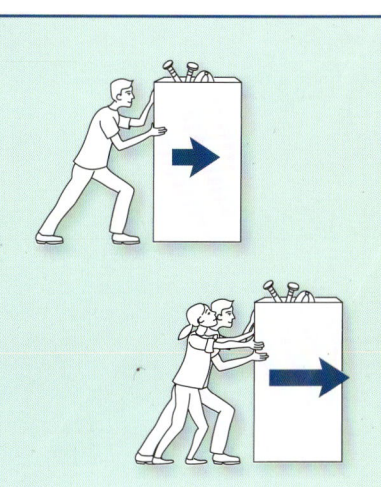

Balanced or Unbalanced?

In a soccer game, the ball is thrown, kicked, and punted. It is often in motion, flying through the air and bouncing on the ground. The ball changes its direction, too, and at times, stops moving.

Remember that all forces have strength and direction. All the forces acting on the ball combine to determine the net force. When the forces on a ball act in opposite directions, the net force is the difference between the forces.

Sometimes, the different forces acting on a ball are balanced. Balanced forces are forces that are the same strength but act in opposite directions. The net force is zero.

When the net force is not zero, the forces are unbalanced. Unbalanced forces cause changes in a ball's motion. The ball might change speed, or direction, or both. The ball moves in the direction of the net force.

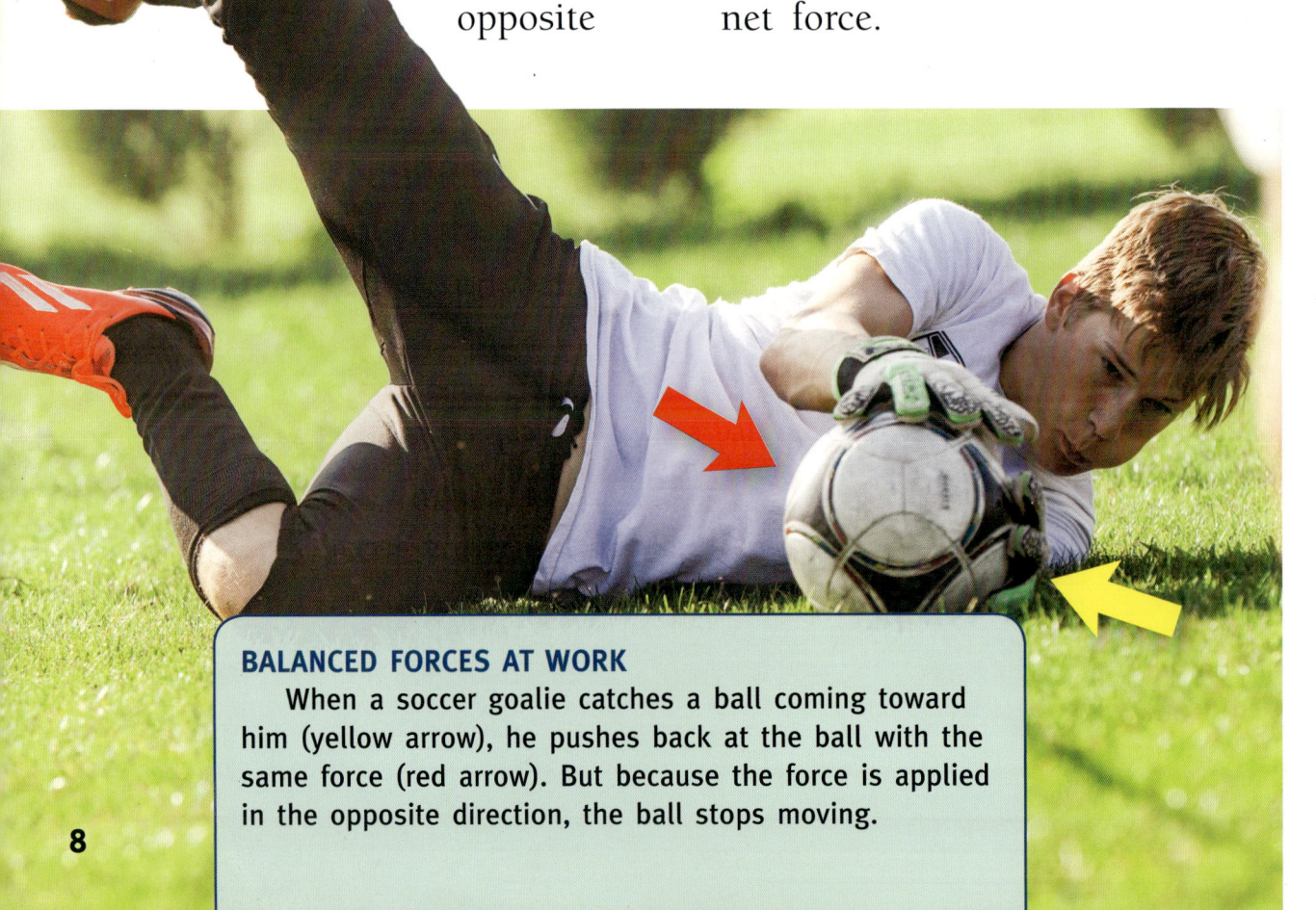

BALANCED FORCES AT WORK
When a soccer goalie catches a ball coming toward him (yellow arrow), he pushes back at the ball with the same force (red arrow). But because the force is applied in the opposite direction, the ball stops moving.

BALANCED FORCES	UNBALANCED FORCES
Net force is equal to zero.	Net force does not equal zero.
An object's motion does not change.	An object's motion changes.
An object that is not moving will stay still.	An object that is not moving will start moving.
An object that is moving will keep moving at the same speed and in the same direction.	An object that is moving will speed up, slow down, or change direction.

UNBALANCED FORCES AT WORK

When a soccer ball is thrown in, the thrower applies a force to it (red arrow). The ball moves in one direction. A player on the other team, however, will try to kick the ball in the other direction. If the defender kicks with more force (yellow arrow) than the incoming throw, the ball will change direction. It moves in the direction of the kick.

9

Dropping and Stopping

In a kickoff in football, the ball flies high in the sky. The ball goes higher and higher in the air. Then the ball's motion changes. It stops for a moment in midair. Then it starts falling back toward the ground. What force is changing the ball's motion?

What about a football that is bouncing and rolling after it lands? Its motion changes, too. It slows down as it rolls. What force is changing its motion?

Objects usually have more than one force acting on them. Changes in motion happen when those forces are unbalanced. The ball in the air changes direction. It moves downward when the force pulling down is greater than the force pushing upward. A rolling ball slows down when the force pushing it backward is bigger than the force pushing it forward.

Gravity is a force that pulls a football downward.

Gravity is a force that pulls objects down. When a ball's motion changes direction and it falls back to the ground, it's because of gravity.

Friction is a force that acts between objects that are

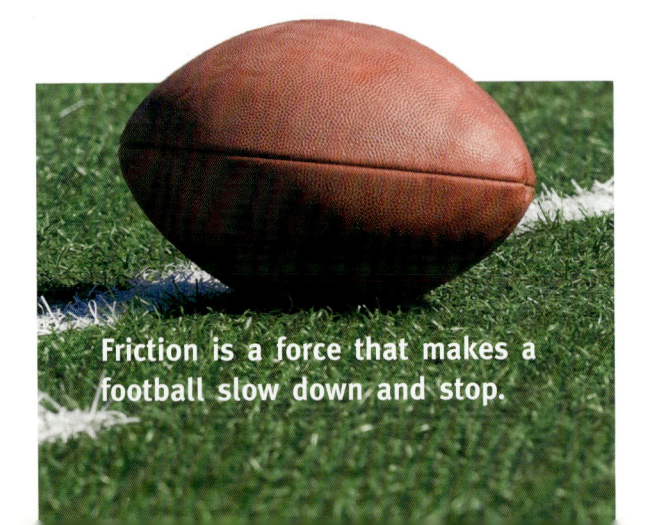

Friction is a force that makes a football slow down and stop.

touching. When a ball rolls over a grassy field, friction changes its motion. It makes the ball slow down and finally stop.

Forces are everywhere in kick-the-ball games on the playground—and everywhere else. Kicking and throwing are two ways that people exert forces on a ball. Friction and gravity are forces that act on the ball, too. Whether the ball is rolling, flying, being kicked, or being caught, forces are in action when people play ball.

Friction: A Helpful Force

Athletic shoes are made so that friction between the playing surface and the shoe keeps the wearer from slipping.

PLAYGROUND PATTERNS

Swings go back and forth. Seesaws go up and down. Merry-go-rounds and other spinning rides go around and around. A playground is full of equipment that moves in patterns.

▲ You can observe many patterns of motion on a playground.

Motion is a change in an object's position. "Back and forth, back and forth" are words that tell about a pattern of motion. In this pattern, moving forward is always followed by moving backward. Then the pattern repeats.

"Up and down, up and down" are words that tell about the pattern of motion of a seesaw. Riders on either side go up and then go down. This motion happens over and over in a pattern.

"Around and around" tells about the motion of a spinner. Riders on the spinner go around and around in a circle. This is another pattern of motion.

The motion of a swing can be changed using forces. If a child on the swing pumps his or her feet, the forward motion of the swing will be bigger. That is followed by a bigger swing backward, too. Riders on a seesaw can push with their feet. The push is a force that can make the seesaw go higher or faster. Riders on the spinner can push, too. They will move in the same direction, but they will go faster and faster!

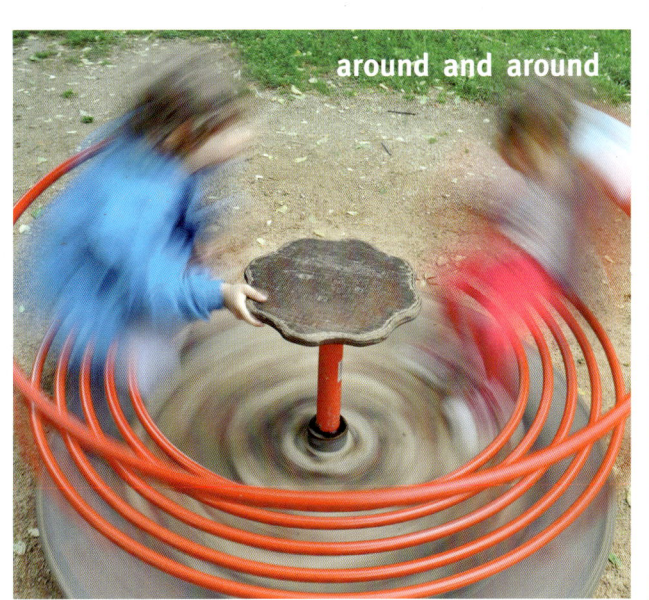

around and around

back and forth

up and down

Measuring and Observing

Motion can be observed and measured. Observation of motion can be used to identify patterns. Measurements can provide even more information about patterns of motion.

What observations and measurements might be helpful for learning about motion?

Here are some ideas:

- how many seconds it takes a swing to go back and forth

- how far up and down a seesaw moves

- how many seconds it takes a spinner to go around once

Measurements can be used to learn about patterns of motion.

What are some questions that could be answered by observing and measuring motion?

- Does the amount of time for one swing back and forth change when a rider stops pumping his or her legs?

- If the seesaw riders do not push with their feet, how many up-and-down motions will happen before they stop moving?

- How does the motion of the spinner change when the riders drag their feet on the ground?

Measuring Motion

Distance is an amount that tells how far an object has moved. The units that are used to measure distance include meters and kilometers (yards and miles). Speed tells how fast an object's motion is. Some units used to describe speed are meters per second and kilometers per hour.

To find an object's speed, the distance traveled and the time it took must both be measured. For example, if the boy in the picture runs 100 meters in 20 seconds, his speed is 5 meters per second.

▲ A stopwatch is used to measure time.

The Motion of a Swing

The pattern of motion of a playground swing is similar to that of a pendulum. A pendulum is an object on a string that can swing back and forth. The motion of a pendulum is a pattern. When the object on the string is pulled upward and then released, the force of gravity causes motion of the pendulum. It swings back and forth in a repeating pattern.

◀ Pendulums can be used to learn about motion, forces, and energy.

A pendulum and a playground swing have the same pattern of motion.

Predicting Future Motion

When motion happens in a regular pattern, information about the pattern can be used to predict future motion. The swings and jumping rope are two examples found on a playground.

For example, a girl riding a playground swing sees that other children are waiting for a turn. She stops pumping her feet. Each forward swing grows smaller (has a shorter distance) than the last one. Each backward swing is smaller, too. The distance the swing moves gets smaller and smaller.

By observing how much smaller each swing gets, the girl can predict the number of swings it will take before she stops moving.

One, two, three, you're in. Now jump . . . and jump! A jump rope swings around and around in a pattern. The person jumping predicts just the right time to jump so his feet go over the rope. How does the jumper make this prediction? By understanding patterns of motion!

▲ These children can use the pattern of the swing's motion to predict when the swing will stop.

▲ Understanding patterns of motion helps this boy have a longer turn jumping rope.

17

MEET A PLAYGROUND DESIGNER

Q&A Andolina Vallone is an architect[1] who designs playgrounds. She attended Syracuse University to learn about planning and designing buildings and other structures. We asked her about her work.

Q: Why do you like to design playgrounds?

A: Playgrounds are a place where people can grow and learn. They are a place where people can practice physical skills, like climbing. They can also try out social skills, like taking turns. Playgrounds are a place where people learn to cooperate. I think that is an important skill, too.

I sketch ideas for a playground before I create a design. ▼

---

1. architect—someone who draws plans for houses, buildings, and other structures, and often supervises their construction

Q: What's your favorite part of designing a playground? What's the hardest part?

A: Sketching is my favorite part. It's the most fun. The hardest part is finding creative ways to pack all the ideas and excitement into the space and the budget.

Q: Where do you get your ideas for playgrounds?

A: Believe it or not, they come from children's books and movies! My goal is to plan a playground that will be different and memorable. I want people to visit again and again.

Built for Climbing

This pyramid net, in a play area in Mesa, Arizona, can hold 250 climbers at one time! It is just over 15 meters tall (nearly 50 feet) and about 24 meters wide (79 feet). According to the builder, Dynamo Playgrounds, it is the largest structure of this kind in the world.

Q: What is the most important thing a designer must keep in mind when creating a playground?

A: Safety is always the main consideration. Lots of space has to be allowed at the ends of slides, in front of and behind swings, and above and below seesaws. The motions of playground equipment can be predicted based on their patterns. These patterns help me plan where different equipment can be placed on the playground.

Q: How important is science in the work of a playground designer?

A: A playground designer needs to know science, and engineering, too. For example, platforms need to be strong enough to hold up with lots of children standing and jumping on them.

Playground designers need to understand forces and motion to design safe playground equipment. ▼

Design for the Environment and Fun

When a playground is built, it changes the environment. The Woodland Discovery Playground in Memphis, Tennessee, was designed to fit into its wooded setting. The children of Memphis helped the designers decide what to put into the playground. Shelby Farms Park Conservancy runs the playground. They said, "It sets a new international standard for natural, educational, and environmental play."

Q: How do you choose materials to use in a playground?

A: Steel, plastic, and wood are often used to build playgrounds. But different materials work better in different parts of the country. Wood can rot in very wet climates. Plastic might melt in a hot desert climate!

Q: How do you test your designs?

A: Ideas and designs are tested by playing! Usually, the designer will test ideas early in the design process. If the idea works, a designer might put together a model in a showroom. Then the designer tests the model and looks for ways that the design can be improved. Of course, children are an important part of the testing process. If they don't like a design, or don't have fun when playing, then it's back to the drawing board!

Q: What do you think makes a playground fun?

A: I love playgrounds that have water fountains built right in. They help keep people cool as they play. I also love playgrounds built in trees.

Q: Do you have a favorite playground?

A: My favorite playground of all time is the fort that I built myself underneath an old, low-hanging pine tree in my parents' backyard. Just a few sticks, a rope swing thrown over a branch, and lots of imagination. That's the fuel that makes playgrounds go!

23

GLOSSARY

balanced forces (BA-lenst FORS-ez) *noun* forces on an object that result in a net force of zero

forces (FORS-ez) *noun* pulls or pushes on an object

friction (FRIK-shun) *noun* a force that makes moving objects slow down

gravity (GRA-vih-tee) *noun* a force that pulls objects down

motion (MOH-shun) *noun* a change in an object's position

net force (NET FORS) *noun* the total force acting on an object

pattern of motion (PA-tern UV MOH-shun) *noun* movement that repeats in a way that can be predicted

unbalanced forces (un-BA-lenst FORS-ez) *noun* forces on an object that result in a net force that is not zero

INDEX

architect, 18
balanced, 8–9
design, 18–22
direction, 5–10, 13
force, 4–11, 13, 16
friction, 10–11
gravity, 10–11, 16

kick, 4–11
kickball, 4
materials, 22
measuring, 14–15
motion, 4–6, 8–11, 13–17, 20
net force, 7–9
observing, 14–15, 17

pattern, 12–14, 16–17, 20
pendulum, 16
playground, 11–12, 16–22
predicting, 17, 20
strength, 6, 8
testing, 22
unbalanced, 8–10